The Co

by the same author

An Eagle Each (with David Pownall)
(Arena, 1971)

The Turns of Time
(Hamlet Press, 1982)

Passport to Walk
(Hamlet Press, 1982)

Passport to Walk is also available from Festival Books.

The Compass Points of Loss

Jack Hill

**Festival Books
from The Greyhound**

First published in Great Britain
by Festival Books

© Jack Hill 1996

ISBN 0 9519100 6 X

Cover design by Barry Woodcock
Typography by Agnesi Text Hadleigh Suffolk
Printed by Progressive Printing Leigh on Sea Essex

Festival Books (from The Greyhound)
is an imprint of The Essex Festival Colchester Essex CO4 3SQ

Contents

Poem to a Young Man	1
For the Memory of a Shetland Poet	3
Circus Maximus	5
Old Poet in Mid Yell, Shetland	6
Tight-rope	7
The Lazar-house of San Antón in Corunna Bay	8
For Antón	26
Noia Fiesta	28
Bulls on the Bullfight Club Walls	31
The Art of Making a Sailor's Wooden Clog	32
The Ship	34
Na terra chan mais longa	35
It was a town by a river	37
From Dusk to Dawn of a Spring Night with Three Bottles of Beaujolais	39
Prising my head from the pillow	67
Dark Dream	68
Of a Certain Age	69

Poem to a Young Man
for Xosé Luís Méndez Ferrín

> *Heureux qui, comme Ulysse, a fait un beau voyage,*
> *ou comme celui-là qui conquit la toison*
> *et puis est retourné, plein d'usage et raison,*
> *vivre entre ses parents le reste de son âge!*

When you return to Aston Flamville-cum-Burbage
having visited numberless lands, eaten other foods
and spoken other languages when confident with wine,
you will see things smaller and shyer, the big houses
only cottages, and the dogs you were afraid of will be dead,
as will the bull and the geese, their heirs
mere puppies and lap-dogs.

When you return to Aston Flamville-cum-Burbage
having walked the stony sierra and climbed the mountains of ice,
you will have in your head the rows of shining boning-knives
and the great scrubbed sawdusty block and the striped apron,
feel elusively on your tongue the pickled walnuts
from the gallon stoneware jars and the bite of the Stilton
from your uncle's dusty thrall, you will smell the brewer's yeast
and the apple wine, and the prickles on your hands
as you gathered sloes and brambles for the gin and the pies
will bleed again, and the soft white fur in the broad bean pods
will come back to your fingertips like a delicate ghost,
and the skills of thrift and preservation and forage, the bones
of your family, will catch on the shoulder of your jacket
like a rosehip sucker and scratch your face
and your eyes will water with salt.

When you return to Aston Flamville-cum-Burbage
in a cold and apple-bearing autumn you will see the birds
squabbling in the Conference pear tree and the brussels in the allotment
and you will go down into the cellar with its barrels and beams

and the spiders will scuttle as their webs brush your face
and a cold kiss will plant its lips of ice on your neck
as distant voices whisper and rustle among the shabby crates
of newspaper-wrapped Coxes and shallots in vinegar
saying 'You have travelled in exile and faced your enemies
and the greatest was yourself' and 'Do you remember the field
of barley where we made love?' and 'My short-horns plodded
for home from the brook past this barn' and 'On the mountains
of Cassino did you see my body?' and 'As you bought your poppy
in Thiepval could you read my name and number?' and you will know
that your voyage is endless and began in the green archaic light
of distant centuries and you will find the hamlet of your grandfather
only in your past and in your future and your uncle only in your mind
and the church will be tiny with no one there you know,
and you will have to go away again with no golden fleece
and with no Troy taken.

When you return to Aston Flamville-cum-Burbage
your grandfather will smile from a corner of the churchyard
and ask 'Have you conquered what you are, have you gathered
events like roses to settle replete with wisdom
in the tutelary intimate fields of your knowledge?'
and you will know that the sun will keep spinning round
its roulette wheel of time away from the birds and the pear tree,
that you come to bury your dead and the dead you bury
will be yourself and your card will fall from the deck
on to a different and totally impersonal baize
and it will be later, so very much later,
and you will not return to Aston Flamville-cum-Burbage then.

For the Memory of a Shetland Poet

The green tide lugs its cargo of crystal up the narrow finger of the voe,
the high taut sails triangulate the blue wind, seals bob and snort
and spit like wine-buffs in the surge, and a menacing arctic skua wheels
like a boomerang round the lighthouse;
walking later on Unst, an old woman, check-aproned, elbows cuddling
    a gate,
on the road back from the memorial to the drowned fishermen calls
'Ah ken wha ye'er. Ye'ere the Englishman biding with Billy Tait
    on Yell' –
we take a dram in the cluttered and polished memories of the croft,
talking of whaling and fleets and murderous winds and loss, and she
    performs
the ritual of reckoning kin. There is an early spring regatta,
and, in the evening, snow.

Drink and women have been the salvation of many a man.

I call to mind your cottage, with its chaos of poems and chessboards,
Villon and Billie Holiday, Walton, Monk, a brace of half-defrosted
    grouse,
cigars and Senior Service, Beaujolais, Beefeater, the rubble-trouble
of clothes piled up on the stairs from which you unerringly tottered
    immaculate,
like a voluble dapper butterfly from a midden, talking of Keats and
    Astaire and the blitz,
of many a five o'clock in the morning, of your marriages, your verse.

You made the circle of your roots to land back upon your Shetland
    feet,
walking as dainty as a cat around the kitchen, sniffing the sea,
exotic, half-gypsyish in face and yet pure Norse, high-cheekboned, wry,
a glass of malt in hand, always a joke, and yet I wonder –
did the island shrink, the doors begin to slam more tightly in your head
and the winter fire burn colder in your eyes, the noose begin to strangle,

and the long-worn, long-loved cravat begin to chafe, to eat into
 the neck?
Islands can be cruel, those lines of voe and sail, of sand and stack and
 harrow,
as the coulter and tractor, net and gaffe co-mesh to make a spider's web,
the bounds of home become mere bonds as the delusions wake
and all the quarters of the wind, of Whalsay and Fladderbister,
Fetlar and Foula and Skerries and Yell shrink to the nails and the
 sponge and the spear,
the soft women vanish to banshees and the Glenfiddich curdles
in the straitjacketed croft you left for the ward in Aberdeen to die.

Out of the heart, out of the mind and the heaving sea
cut the black rocks of shipwreck, throwing the broken tanker
to the indifferent staining sand and the throttled kittiwake;
caught in the shrieking winds of the past, the evil-eyed faces
of the manuscript demons, Atimo, Radamas, Asmodeus, Modo and
 Mahu
and Obidicut growl and sneer in the night, and rattle their dirty claws
against the window, threatening treachery, disfigurement, and pain,
and the croft of retirement caves in, and the drugs
banish the horrors of the Apocalypse to a numb tepidity
and in the end to nothing
                              Oh my friend of so much laughter,
Oh my friend I fear and grieve your ending, I pray for your soul
and hope there was an escape hatch, a fail-safe door, a bolt-hole
you found, to leave your tired mind like a forgotten rag,
take your body back to Yell to sleep by the voe with its seals
and urge your newly nascent spirit to the vociferous laughing sky where

Drink and women have been the salvation of many a man.

Circus Maximus

The tension of columns
moves into a line; a cord
sustains the poise of a man
on a string, a breathing
vulnerable entablature.

The circus is a frieze
where, sculptured by spotlights,
pole-centred, he walks
deftly over the stressed air,
as the gods sit to see,
hoping and fearing for
the fall of man.

He does not fall.

Tomorrow he will not fall again
in his tented temple;
the rocking columns bear the load,
surrounded by hemlock and mint.

Old Poet in Mid Yell, Shetland

He walks along the cliff edge,
fearing to fall, but drawn
to the deep sea: scared
of the height, of the houses
marking out their spaces
of light, as a fox marks out
its territory with piss.

Ducking the day he hopes
for sunset.

The mistress he covets now
has no arms or womb,
comes every night,
is black, and does not sing.

Tight-rope

That the ghosts come
in their holy company
he is half aware,
carrying the balancing cross,
less afraid of them
than of the living;
he talks to the dead
and hates the doctor –
the friends he drank with
are gone; a single
glass is poured for all;
by one precise cliff edge
he walks between the worlds
and does not fall.

The Lazar-house of San Antón in Corunna Bay

In memoriam Antón Avilés de Taramancos, detained in the lazar-house after it had become a gaol, and whom I last saw in the cancer ward of Corunna hospital, by which time the former lazar-house, quarantine station and gaol had become an archaeological museum.

I

□

There is a stone
        in the prison,
a hefty cube
        about 8" × 8" × 8"
(naturally of granite)
        mounted on a revolving pedestal.
On its four lateral faces
        are carved
four primitive faces
        indecipherably weathered:
eerie deities
        looking at and guarding
the entrances
        which are also the exits
to the town
        to the crossroads,
    the central place
    which cannot be seen
    the fourth dimension.

II

The granite island hulks
        in the water
defensively architectured
        as a star-fort.
Its four mutations
        imitate the wind's quarters,
north, south, east, west –
        lazar-house, quarantine,
gaol, museum
        the crossroads of tide,
crossways of the witch,
        the four seasons,
birth, youth, age, death,
        the labyrinth of the umbilical
sailing to a black bull
        in the axed Galician night.
'Eu son da costa do morte'
        – I am from the coast of death –
says the smiling guide.
        The punishment cell
is full of Celtic gold,
        intricate torques,
dense-worked jewellery
        behind the bars.
'Nine months I spent here'
        laughed my old friend.
'A magic number,
        a life number.'
Nine months in the four-
        walled cell

            in the compass-boxed gaol,
                        in the wet stone walls
            where the lepers died
                        of their disease,
            the sailors quarantined,
                        the captives held
                  without trial.

III

Earth, air, fire, water –
        but there is little earth
in the star-fort,
        little can grow.
The labyrinth conceals
        its beast or prisoner,
is apt for death
        not harvest,
preserves the grave-goods,
        the jewels of the underworld
sacrificed to grow
        imaginary corn
by the salt shoulders
        of the desperate sea.
Even on a hot day the air
        in the cells is damp.
'I am from the coast of death'
        says the smiling guide,
'from the end of the earth.'
        She is twenty-three or so,
and her boyfriend is waiting
        on the harbour wall.
This was the house
        of illness, of quarantine,
which has now been removed
        up the hill to the hospital
past the Outeiro,
        the steep road
which links the places
        of confinement

    the cell and ward
           split by thirty-six years –
the four suits and seasons
           multiplied by nine of womb,
an amniotic time,
        a cruciform destination
from the water here
        to the earth by the sea
of the rías baixas
       where he was born
     and where he now is buried.

IV

☐

From the lazar-house
        is seen the graveyard
of Sir John Moore
        and in the graveyard
underneath the elm trees
        is his tomb
like all tombs
        rectangular,
a human geometry
        mocked by the grave
waves of the sea.

V

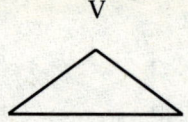

There is always a softness to the clear white marble and to the bronze, to the melting forms of Giambologna whom I so much admire, a softness even palpable in the Vatican virgin of Michelangelo, visible certainly in the David. In Bernini's fountains and gold, in the formal assertions of Brunelleschi. Organized pasta. Proportions of the lute-string, the precious theory. Granite does not yield, and years ago I walked three hundred kilometres over granite mountains to a serious granite city. Now I live by the sea, by the home of the labyrinthine crab, the intransigent oyster, the spiralled whelk and winkle, painstakingly nutritious. Hard-shelled food for the harsh-voiced gull. The intractable. Destructible, if at all, only by the formless sea. A land supportive of gorse, of pine. With Inca-like façades, turning and scrolling upwards to the sky in their musculate paternity of stone, wizard faces looking all ways at once, enduring nearly for ever.

The sea. The gaol. The dice. The lazar-house.

VI

'The spiral is the purest form of movement.'
Paul Klee

No. Klee was wrong. The spiral is a holy form, a magic form, a prehistoric form. But not pure in its movement. It is the form of the intestine, the labyrinth, the subterranean burial chamber, the whirlpool. It is worshipped not for its purity, but for its danger. It is placated, not loved. If it leads to an afterlife it leads through dissolution, demolition, dung. The compost of history. It is adored by, guarded by, and guards, witches and monsters. Its instruments are the French horn, the tuba. It is deaf to the angels with their harps and strings. Its totem, the snail. It strips like wire. The palaeolithic hunters knew this, and scratched it on rocks. It lasts; has teeth, a vulva, a sword. At the centre of the spiral is a handful of damp earth, studded with fragments of Celtic or pre-Celtic bone. Inconceivably old. A dead bull. A broken torque.

A herb growing from the eye socket of a wolf.

VII

    The crossroads.

Upon the platform
        below the quadrifaz
at the crossroads
        were laid the coffins
of the Celtic dead
        that they should say
their last farewell
        to the roads of the earth
    the revolving earth.

Each face, each Herm –
        does it protect or menace,
attract the arrival
        or thrust him back?
It is not a moral
        but a warning,
evoking expulsion
        or welcome.

    Stay, or turn back.
    The choice is yours.

VIII

'Which is the best way to Cork?'
'If I was you I wouldn't start from here.'

Through this harbour passed
        Drake and John of Gaunt,
Hugh Roe O'Donnell
        after the battle of Kinsale,
and the great Armada,
        the invincible Armada
towards its Irish storm,
        passed boatloads
of starving rachitic exiles
        from the Galician famine,
the British army
        after its chaotic retreat,
Philip the Second
        for his useless Tudor marriage
and Charles the First
        to be crowned
as Emperor
        in Aquisgrán.
In this harbour
        stayed lepers, the plagued,
the prisoners of San Antón
        – patron saint of the diseased,
of animals,
        preacher to the fish –
stayed until death
        rowed from his coast

         with an incurious smile
                  to earn his ferryman pennies.
         As the Armada found
                  and so did the British,
         the road there is also
                  the road back,
         the crossroad
                  and the spiral
            lead to the same place.

IX

From here left the great armies
        to here returned the ruined ships.
The emperor's coronation
        and the dead salt marriage.
Even the name of the place
        is obscure, tends towards the shadow.
Corunna, Colonia in Latin,
        or Columna from its lighthouse,
or Corín, the Celtic
        for an isthmus, an outcrop.
Three names, not four.
        The fourth, its dark and secret name,
    known only to Dis.

X

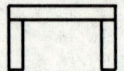

In the cell there was
        a New Testament.
Let us name the voices.
        St Matthew, the angel
who guides and guards,
        who dictates.
St Mark, the lion of Venice,
        the voice sounding the depths
of the desert and sea.
        St Luke, the painter, the ox
dragging his cart of coloured stone.
        St John, the eagle,
the apocalyptic, the royal,
        the high-winged bird.
St Paul, the epistolar,
        bearing his fatal sword.
But this is the place of the shell,
        the land of St James,
the hard salt shell
        imprisoning the vulnerable flesh,
place of the rapping pilgrim staff,
        of the endless blistered road.
Where is the gospel of the carapace,
        the bivalve,
the mollusc, the barnacle,
        where is the evangel of the crab?
Here, in the star-fort,
        in whose granite
even the spiral ammonite
        cannot be found,

>   on whose black blocks
>   ring voices of the dead, the waves.
> Here it is the work of older man,
>   a petroglyph
> chipped into the rock
>   by a caveman or druid,
> an act of will, like pilgrimage,
>   which holds forever tight
> the flesh and the round
>   spiral of ocean and road,
> trigonometric time
>   beneath the changing clouds.
>   The lazar-house. The gaol.

XI

☐

The legends are dark
        in this city of net-makers,
clog-cutters, coal-coasters,
        eviscerators of fish,
gatherers of percebes
        in the vicious waters
dying year by year
        for their luxury harvest,
city of tar-boilers, chandlers,
        granite-carvers, ships.
Here we start
        with a decapitation,
a light, and, as always,
        a hero.
Hercules, after a three-day
        three-night battle
buried the head of Geryon
        – ter amplium Geryonen –
on the promontory,
        and erected a tower.
And here, above the pulverized skull,
        high in the tower,
still burns the light,
        the Pharos,
oldest in Europe,
        marking the city,
given its inevitable
        granite-blocked seal
by Caius Servius Lupus,
        the Portuguese wolf, the builder,

after a thousand years
    of Phoenician flame.
Farr, in the Viking tongue,
    Pharos, no change.
North, South, East, West.
    The place of labours,
of business done
    in great waters,
in the toils of death,
    the decapitation
of cod, hake, tunny.
    The tin, the copper, the gold.
Cornwall, Carthage, Rome.
    Place of cabin boys and harpooners.
Of exile. Still.

XII

θ

Chronos
        expelled from the time
of godhead
        to the slower pulse
of seals, shrimps, mud.
        Or Cruña, the woman
who gave birth
        after the decapitation.
Invisible from the gaol
        is the great beacon
telling of the bay
        warning of the rocks,
lighthouse
        of a million sailings.
Near the lighthouse
        is the new gaol,
soon, in its turn,
        to be closed,
converted to a museum
        of fish and fishing,
(prisoners moved again
        past the steep hill
towards the mountain)
        a museum to exhibit
the history of turbot and herring,
        percebe, cockle, lobster.
Farr and far
        is the pharos, the light
of this uncathedralled city,
        in this long run
of water and algae.

             In the beginning,
– fiat lux et facta est –
                burning, burning,
North, South, East, West,
                visible from the hillside,
invisible from the gaol,
                the revolving head
so far from Rome
                which on slaved foundations
built it above
                the bloody decapitation,
the great Phoenician fire.
                Who has, who knows
the true name?
                How many names and deaths?
        The light flashes. The tide ebbs.
                Both turn.

For Antón

       Conforming to the tides like weed, or throbbing
on a rock like oysters is safe, though vulnerable
to all the pollutions that appear within the bay – fish
vanish, or die, and the hard-faced cocklers lose
their prize and go back home with empty sacks:

difficult waters, the human soul, where things
are lost, the timbers crack, the sails split
and the tide table is unknowable, the pilot drunk,
and the purser has already legged it with the gin
before you hit the rocks;
                       difficult waters
in which we have no choice but flinch
or sail, skim the white horses on towers
of air or turn our backs on the wind
to spit at a cooling grate –
                           oh the white horses
born so far away, rolling and growling
to the dangerous haven where they shatter
in an end of spray and diamond, which we have
to row like men, and bleed upon the sliding seat
beneath us as we pant or die, to strike
and feather for the giant causeway
which we fear and need, like you, the poet
in the sea-voiced shell,
a rhythmic face wrinkled by love and words,
a galley slave bound to his own and chosen oar.

You, like many other friends from distant places
speaking odd languages, are more of myself
than my simple relations, my normal boundaries;
have asked, and given, more than the man
next door, simple and honourable and here,
have seen and spoken of more, of jaguars

and amethysts, of topaz castles in the Inca air,
of new wine and moistened mouths of love,
departures and returns, the sexual pulse
of the Atlantic clenching its dampened thighs
about the Spanish shore, have provided,
like an otter or an eagle, or the salt-blasted shield
of a dead conquistador, a glimpsed flash
of some strange curiosity or magnificence.
                To all voyages,
of which you know many, there is a harbour
with odd-looking people talking various tongues:
after all voyages there is a harbour
made of water where the granite floats,
and the wind is made of home, the vegetables fresh,
and the wine clear in the bright and friendly bars.
                As you sail through the soil
beside the water, and tack your passage
through the pregnant rock towards the fiery heart,
send me a shanty or hymn to mock the silence,
a joke to dance the sea-pinks by the cliff,
sell me a fake ruby with a truthful rhyme
and a straight face:
                              write me, with your normal
humorous pause, your cabin boy's dead reckoning
of the stars.

Noia Fiesta

arrivals, departures, returns

Caught in the circle of the mountains,
mauve flowers growing on the façade
of a once religious past, its future
snarled with traffic and noise
and foreign languages, the town stands
on granite toes to almost see the sea,
humping on sparkling stone shoulders
a sackful of boats and half-ruined pazos,
fishheads and pubs and letters from Cuba,
coats-of-arms, mud, discothèques, little dogs,
passports and sardines and political posters,
itinerant wizards, gypsies with goats, Atlantic breezes
pulling against the shrouds of bluest air
punctuated by gulls, crosses, mussel shells,
and the smell of the sierra on fire
drifting a eucalypt purgatory of black ash
down to the heedless water, and grips its jewels
and its rubbish in a labyrinth of sea,
a friendly Minotaur awaiting the axe
or lying in wait with one.

After Mass there will be a session of vermouth.
Mullets swim past the slaughterhouse
and I talk in the bar to the poet with the face
that had heard, but not believed,
all the Jehovah's Witnesses since Jericho,
of a dead Polish priest called Popieluscko
to whose funeral I went, heavy in leather and wool,
eight years ago in a great city of darkness
far from the sea, lost among the snow,
the secret police, and the chrysanthemums,
queuing for the holy bread of witness

as the women queued each morning
for the holier bread of life outside the empty shops,
as a man might queue or pray for love
in the terror of a sea in storm, for refuge,
for harbour, hope, for air, for respite
from the endless Penelope's loom of journeys,
the ceaseless preponderant enlacement
of the tide that drives us on, the ocean-turbine
sluicing its cargo of bread and octopus
up the ría and back, and up and back
towards the granite town, offering
an embrace (is it?) or a stranglehold.

Mauve flowers grow on the church façade,
decorations on the stationary axle of Tapal,
its square emptied of priests and movement,
housing now, apart from the dogs, a bank,
a vacuum, and a bar, mauve flowers
thrown into the interstices of stone
by an impossible, mythic wave, setting
their carnal roots into the Celtic strata,
twining and kissing above the darkened aisle.
I think of Popieluscko and Mishima, the dead,
the murdered priest, the seppuku bard,
of Warsaw and Tokyo, places where my feet
have been to seek redemption from the wheel,
my hands have fingered sea-strings of an old guitar
I cannot play, and I have heard the guttural vowels
as of gulls along the streets, have drunk sake and vodka,
gulped raw fish and beetroot, listened,
like a helmsman, to the screaming wind
among the ropes, or sacrificed to Venus
who so often gripped and so inviolable
remains the sea in which we swim,
stubborn, afraid, and needing, to the town
of stone and flowers, the diction
of complicated architecture made of bone,

this tree of blood and knowledge drowning
in the ocean's black and soft recess
or sculptured in the glittering noisy air.

Bars and sea, Noah, sailor and drunkenness,
Venus, goddess of oysters, pearls, and fleets.
It is always the goddesses who are watchers
and porters at the gates of life and death,
Magdalene at the tomb, Lucina
at the birth, the washers and the layers-out,
skilled to shave the dead or cut the cord,
keepers of the sea on which we merely sail,
lovely as Venus or as foul as Hecate, making
the blood we spill, and spilling their blood
like moons across the seas they rule.

Multas per gentes et multa per aequora vectus,
I walk at four o'clock in the morning
thinking of all who shipped and lost their ship,
of those whom Venus did not save, the Palinuruses
without an epic who came from, came to,
and left again from here.
I go to sleep beside the ría,
wake into the sun, and walk towards the church
with the mauve flowers, the bank,
and the bar, and think of all the other rites
and dreams that flowered and lost themselves
within the ring of granite and the sapphire stones
of sea and mud, this small fish-headed town
that never moves and is never still,
to which the sailor owes his sacrifice
as to his Venus or his Minotaur,
the goddess and the god, the oysters and the bull,
the flower, the net, the labyrinth, the sea,
the fiesta, our blood.

Bulls on the Bullfight Club Walls

Huge black heads line the wall: their names, their breeders,
how many horses killed so many years ago.

Beneath them, grey-haired men play cards and chatter
– the cost of living, the cost of tickets –
and the past's rare, crimson, brilliant afternoons
are poorly preserved in the fading signed photographs
on the other wall, Gallo, Manolete, Ordoñez, Esplà.

As the old men laugh and slap the dusty green cloth
(three of them, now in jeans, slacks, and a suit respectively,
have worn the lights, carried the sword,
undergone the wounds) six hundred miles south
of this cold gulled city, in the gathering heat
of an Andalucian spring, two-year-olds
grow powerful, beautiful, and lower their heads beneath the cork trees
to test their horns.

The Art of Making a Sailor's Wooden Clog

The foot of the sailor is by nature broad,
with widely spaced toes, used to planting its sole
on the softness of sand. A touch
so sensitive that it knows when it treads on tide line,
on pebble, weed, or rush. It is a sounding plumb
to transmit the condition of the sea: temperatures,
flows, breaking waves. The barometer of time. Signal
of abundant fish, or where the sea
bottoms beyond the ría.
The foot of the sailor is another song.

To make a clog for this measure, to construct
something to protect a living fragile structure
which is at the same time as strong as a tree stump or an anvil block
is a labour of skill. You must compose yourself,
measure with an osier twig the curvature, the instep,
the proportion, the length, the space
in which the foot finds freedom, or in which – after labour –
the foot walks dry, painfully, unwilling
to know of anything more.

You have to
find a willow tree by a river,
fairly slender-rooted, mature;
and, while the moon is waning, when the sap does not have
the force which sings in the arteries of the bole,
cut it down with a Portuguese saw, having inserted the correct wedges
so that it knows the proper angle to fall.

Once it has been well trimmed, select from the crown
that tone of wood with a tint
between a salmon red and a Finisterre sunset,
a somewhat narrow range, difficult to explain
(almost always, if you tap it with a knuckle, the willow

responds with the clack of a primitive drum, the magical
and millennial noise which awakes a shiver
in the fountains of the blood. Atavisms, maybe.) And then
split the trunk dead centre. Into the sun to weather
– not in the moonlight which twists the grain –
for just seven days. Not one more.

Take the adze, the gouge, the most delicate jig-saw,
the broad file: on one of those calm evenings
when the smoke moves gently after a storm,
roll yourself a cigarette, very slowly, and sketch
on the wood, lightly now, the design;
only now can you cut it, make a convex-concave base,
measure the exact ellipse, and now
we have the perspective of the sailor's clog . . .

The rest is fine detail, trivial matters,
unidimensional art.

From the Galician of Antón Avilés

The Ship

On the other side of the bay they are building a ship:
the hammering of the shipwrights echoes in the morning,
and they do not know that they are building
the glass tower of my infancy. They do not know
that each part, each plank and timber,
is part of my being, do not know
that in the heart of the keel is the very marrow
of my spinal column: that the smouldering pitch
is the magic perfume of life.
When at the launching they hoist the sail, and the rigging
trembles softly in the air,
it will be my heart that feels the wind,
it will be my heart.

From the Galician of Antón Avilés

Na terra chan mais longa

In the longest stretch of land,
endlessly long, terribly long,
circular, stretched like a steel drum
where the sun is neither father, brother, nor friend
but a travelling sinister thug
thoughtlessly crushing the temperate bones –
in the land of the xoropo, the jaguar, papaya,
on the banks of the Vichada, the Guaviare, the Meta,
in the heart of the jungle, at the heart of the world,
one thousand five hundred kilometres from man,
came full of mist to visit me the sea.

And I cried like a man, like a trapped wolf:
I cried not from anguish, from love or from anger,
but the cry of a distant badly wounded tiger,
the breaking-out of the man of the sea whom one day
I had buried in the deepest hole of my blood.

The sea came to visit me,
the sea of Finisterre, the sea of Vida,
the older sea of the agile pilot boats
smelling of oily linen, sailing gear,
fish oil, bladderwrack,
fresh foam, tar, chowder,
and my breath was a storm,
and the white milled flour of the ocean settled on the forest
because the sea came to visit me.

The dew of salt quietened my body,
one thousand five hundred kilometres from man:
the friend, the companion of my deepest heart,
the captain of the bright sailing ships,
the happy sea rocking the dinghies,
which I love so much that it will not forget me.

Sailor, one night the two of us will sing
drunk as Ulysses on the jetty of a port,
covered with saltpetre and the south-east wind,
the two of us smelling of sea and freedom and wine,
and the sea will be as happy as a father come home.

One night the two of us will sing so loud a bass
that the most powerful love will erupt,
an atomic love, a unique force
born of tenderness and the shore of the sea.

Today my skeleton is a great dockyard
where come the wounded ships of yesterday,
the high prows of unspotted whiteness
with the names of women, names of roses,
names full of blue and salt and the waves:
– Olga – The Boatman's Flower – Loyalty –
which today the men coarsened by progress
force to sail with diesel and hatred.

(I love the silent packet boats,
the watchful narrow corvettes,
I love the machine in itself,
I love the energy.
But I hate the dark crime
of the assassination of triumphant ships.)

Oh brother sea,
here in the immense seed-bed,
in the immense seed-bed of Vaupes, Casenare,
the honoured embrace of your arm came to me,
and I howled in the jungle transformed
until the salt of tears gave me rest,
a seashore stretched out for my lip.

Based on the Galician of Antón Avilés

It was a town by a river

It was a town by a river.
I won't give its name, though I remember it,
for it is not the name of any town.
The river ran peacefully by, through secret alders
through a golden, sacramental land.
And there was a long avenue, with ambiguous poplars;
and the town was stretched out, long,
long as a slender girl.
Swifts flew round the church.
And the people were quiet, with an ordinary beauty.
And in the doorways, time on their knees,
women sewed the days of their life.

Khaki uniforms, stars on the sleeve.
Not many. I was in charge. I was taking them somewhere.
A halt on the journey, the town was welcoming.
In the easy air, sitting in the café,
we smoked away the evening.

The town was so beautiful, and the river, and the people.
If only we could have stayed.
My men dreamed of settling
with the slender, virtuous girls
for ever.
And of talking to the old women coming out of church,
talking courteously.
And of going out hunting, of hunting good partridge
with well-mannered men.

But the next day we had to go.

From the Galician of Ricardo Carballo Calero

**From Dusk to Dawn
of a Spring Night
with Three Bottles of Beaujolais**

Twenty-six Dodoitsu

The dodoitsu is a song, often but not always about love. It has four lines, of seven, seven, seven and five syllables. It is a satirical, boozy, popular form. Though it shares some characteristics with the more courtly styles of the haiku and tanka (it, like them, is based on syllable quantity), it, unlike them, is available for the slangy, the preposterous, and the irreverent, as well as for the elegiac and the seasonal. Variety and incongruity are its elements, and though it lacks high seriousness this does not imply that it need be facetious. Only its form is consistent – consistency in time and theme would be untrue to the dodoitsu, as they are indeed to life itself. The ingenuous as well as the ingenious can live in it.

1

I stepped on to the Boeing
727 smiling
with my duty-frees, my bag,
and an erection.

2

I like Spain. The cooking's crap,
the noise is unbearable,
the sun's too hot, the cold's worse,
and yet, I like Spain.

3

The dawn breaking, the cointreau,
the tiny airless bedroom.
Her tongue in my ear. My hands
clenched in her dark hair.

4

She arched her back, and giggled.
She leaned forward, closed her mouth
upon me. The seagulls mewed.
Red flesh. The white wine.

5

I'm certain she was a cat.
She knew the future, had claws,
and used them, fucked, and her eyes
glowed in the darkness.

6

Yes, she was a cat. Ate fish
and oysters, went out at night
and moved in total silence.
She hunted, not danced.

7

I loved her, but I feared her.
She was stunning in the sack.
She was a witch with Tarot.
I was a coward.

8

She tried to poison herself.
I remember cold white breasts
and jet-black hair. Limp hands. Blood,
brown eyes and vomit.

9

The dark incompatibles:
her husband, my mistress. Miles,
wine and beer. Her blood, my lies.
My England. Her Spain.

10

I saw her by the graveside,
with her children. None of them
looked at me. Others cried. We didn't.
He was dead. Like us.

11

It's a bitch when you can't eat or drink, don't enjoy screwing, you can't live with her, and you can't sleep without her.

12

I write my postcards, I lick
my stamps. I tell tall stories.
I give my witty lectures.
I'm fun. I'm angry.

13

The sod! She asked me to lunch,
and what did I get? Salad,
an apple, *water*, the cat,
AND her gay brother.

14

Springtime happened yesterday,
with sun, cold beer and kisses –
but now it is raining,
and the girl has gone.

15

Cherry blossom? A cliché.
I like autumn, and bonfires,
leaves, strong Rhône wine, and women
to cuddle at night.

16

Inside the sword museum
on a snarling Tokyo street
sits steel calm on white linen –
such savage beauty.

17

Remembering a movement,
or a meal, a restaurant –
what she said – and one's aplomb
crumples like tinfoil.

18

A hint of the same perfume,
even the same colour dress,
even a place name, and you
remember it all.

19

The most beautiful names? Pubs.
The Wig and Fidget. The Bull.
The Dog and Hedgehog. The Grapes.
The Man in the Moon.

20

The curate is twenty-four.
I am fifty and a bit.
I said, 'Hi!' He said, he *said*,
'Please call me Father.'

21

I love her. We go to bed.
We like similar music.
She dances well. I love her.
I smile. I fear death.

22

Hers. I don't fear my own. Hers.
This is an unknown feeling.
We make love. I make her laugh.
I want her living.

23

An empty house: frayed curtains,
ripped gold wallpaper, and
a dead butterfly rocks in
the spider's hammock.

24

Two common things together
make a durable vision –
a motionless ladybird
on a clean white sheet.

25

Richard, and the gillivors
in the cool Quaker graveyard.
Gerry loved Spanish sailors.
Gone, my dear gay friends.

26

I like the dodoitsu
more than the haiku. It's odd,
unbuttoned. And – admit it –
who needs the cherries?

Prising my head from the pillow

Prising my head from the pillow
with a tremulous crowbar,
I clean my teeth, shave, and meditate
on the heart-felt glory of a night ill-spent.

Dark Dream

I saw a body on a tree
In a dark spinney;
The tree was a hazel,
The body my son's.

I saw a body in a lake
In a dark spinney;
The lake was oval,
The body my father's.

I saw a body on a rock
In a dark spinney;
The rock was limestone,
The body my wife's.

I saw a body in a fire
In a dark spinney;
The fire was oak logs,
The body mine.

The hazel tree of the arms
Lifts no hawk to the air;
The oval lake of the face
Is drained to the bone;
The limestone rock of the spine
Erodes in the rain-swept day;
The oak fire of the blood
Has burned my body away.

Of a Certain Age

Gingko, casuarina, fuchsia,
waratah, oak, lemon tree,
hang up the Noh-play costumes,
shut down the M.C.C.

Scratched is my South Pacific,
lost are the King and I,
I've forgotten the plots of Aida
and Madam Butterfly.

Davison, Condon, Tatum,
have all gone underground –
in the middle of so much music
I've lost my sense of sound.

I pray to the old Madonnas
with neither hope nor tears,
while the rap resounds in the disco
and the roof falls in on my ears.

I've gone off the vintage Médoc,
can't afford Chablis,
don't bother with parsley or pheasant,
oysters that tang of the sea,

oxtail is a delusion,
turbot now is a waste,
my teeth aren't up to a rock cake,
I've lost my sense of taste.

Bocuse, and the Roux, and Olivier
could just as well be hung –
while waiters gabble and snigger,
the fat congeals on my tongue.

Florist carnations and lilies
smell of damp Cellophane –
can't tell the cheese from the butter,
the perfume from the drain.

Lauder, Dior, and Givenchy
might just as well be in hell,
the fluoride's just like the water,
I've lost my sense of smell.

Where are all the old taverns,
what on earth is the point of the rose?
When the wine is dead to the nostril
the emptiness gets up my nose.

Paved are the fields of the Midlands;
pay to enter St Paul's,
you can't see the dome for the tourists,
scaffolding covers the walls.

Katoomba, Kyoto, Galicia,
are visible only in mind,
I can't see as far as my lenses,
I think I'm going blind.

Façades are made out of plastic,
neon scrambles the skies,
the night is full of monoxide,
the sun burns holes in my eyes.

Can't feel the wool from the nylon,
can't tell the hip from the breast,
dog from cat, fish from fowl or fellatio,
can't tell the bra from the vest.

Benetton, Superglue, Jaeger,
I neither finger nor clutch,
no stroking, or far less caressing,
I've lost my sense of touch.

I try to catch running water,
try to get hold of the sand,
as the bones gleam white on my fingers,
and my fingers grow cold on my hand.

The long miles of all of my travels
read like a closed book to me,
and the past retreats like an army
to the oil-bespattered sea –

Gingko, casuarina, fuchsia,
Brisbane, Seville, and Tralee,
hang up the Noh-play costumes,
the bullfight, and cricket, and me.